Living with a Springer Spaniel: Pete and Me

Kathleen McKee

Kathleen McKee

First Edition E-book: June 2016
First Edition Print: June 2018

Cover design by Robin Ludwig Design Inc.
www.gobookcoverdesign.com

ISBN-10: 1719363447
ISBN-13: 978-1719363440

Printed in the United States of America

"A dog will teach you unconditional love. If you can have that in your life, things won't be too bad."

– Robert Wagner

Kathleen McKee

Also by Kathleen McKee

The Poustinia Series:

Poustinia: A Novel
Joyful Encounters
Bountiful Legacies

A Specter of Truth

No Gifts to Bring

Introduction

A friend once asked me about the lifespan of a springer spaniel. I honestly didn't know. At the time, Pete had been with me for about 10 years. I began searching for information about springer spaniels. Oddly, it was something I had never done. In fact, I knew nothing specific about the breed except that they were hunter dogs. And very cute.

There's a wealth of information about springer spaniels on the Web and in books. There are training manuals and guides on how to best care for your pet. There are even reports that can help you decide if a springer would be a good fit for your family. No doubt, these are written by experts who know all aspects of the dog's temperament, heritage, and use in the field.

I don't discount these credible sources. Pete might have turned out differently if I had done some research before I opened my heart and my home to him. But I wouldn't have traded the world for my dog. He was loyal, affectionate, and smart. Pete took care of me, and I took care of him. At least that's what I told him every day. It worked for us.

My dad had a heartwarming portrait of an old man sitting by a large hearth with a springer spaniel lying at his feet. Dad loved that picture and told me that he often cogitated—that's what he'd say—about the good old days. The scene was one he could imagine as he lived out his senior years.

I wasn't too surprised when dad called me one day and said, "I found a springer spaniel in the paper. AKC Registered. Only 100 bucks." I *was* surprised when he added, "You want it?"

I told dad that I thought he should get the puppy, as he often spoke about the one in the picture he treasured so much. He reminded me that he was a snowbird and lived in Florida for 6 months of the year. "Yeah, but the other 6 months you have a home with ten acres of woods," I argued.

"Can't do it," he said. "I think you ought to get it."

I knew Dad wanted that springer, but he recognized the challenges of a lengthy drive at least twice a year with an active dog in the car. I agreed to purchase him. Dad would pick out which puppy *I* might like of the litter, and *we* would get a male, so *we* could breed him. That was Dad's plan and, believe it or not, I went along with it.

I bought all kinds of puppy stuff. I got a nice travel kennel since I'd have to drive the puppy back to my home, about 3 hours away. I got the bowls, food, toys, bed, collar, leash, and training pads. By that point, I excitedly waited for the call to come get him.

Dad selected the best of the litter, he told me. He decided that we should name him Pete. But on his papers, we'd call him Sir Peter of Archbald. I thought Pete was a good name for a dog, so that was fine with me.

The day finally arrived for me to come get Pete and take him to my home. At 6 weeks of age, Pete was the cutest bundle of fur I ever saw. He had mahogany brown ears, with a white muzzle and crown. His body was white with dark brown patches, speckled with freckles, particularly on his nose and arms. He was docked so there was only a nub of a brown tail. It was love at first sight.

I recently did some research and learned that springer spaniels have a life-span of 12-15 years. Pete didn't quite make it that long, but almost. We were pals for 11 years, and it broke my heart when he went to doggie heaven on a frigid day after a March blizzard in 2017. It was much too soon.

I want to share my story about Pete for several reasons. Not just because he was my special boy. That's a given. But more for all that Pete taught me. I learned the rules of doggie ownership. I learned traits of the breed. One step at a time; often by the seat of my pants because I had never met another springer owner. Not ever, in the entire 11 years Pete and I were together. I also didn't know there are Facebook groups devoted to springer spaniels. How I wish I'd had those members as mentors when Pete was with me.

Nonetheless, I experienced my springer on a day-to-day basis, gaining more knowledge than had I merely studied a manual. Perhaps, in some ways, Pete was the teacher. He showed me what he liked and disliked, what he was thinking, and what qualities are inherent in his breed. All I had to do was watch and listen. Pete taught me everything I needed to know.

Living with a Springer Spaniel might help you decide if a springer would be a good addition to your family, or if there are characteristics of the breed that you wouldn't find acceptable. Although each pup is unique, I now know that Pete exhibited all of the traits that are common to springers. Springer spaniels are friendly, loyal, smart, and eager to please. And they spring! Here's what I learned.

Rule #1:

Initiate Training Immediately

Pete and I enjoyed the day getting to know one another before it was time to leave for my home in Archbald, PA. We played and cuddled, seeming to have bonded immediately. Nonetheless, Pete didn't expect to take a trip. He was shaking as I zippered him into his travel kennel and worked to hook the contraption up to my car's back seat seatbelt. He was whimpering as I began the long drive, so I turned on the car radio, thinking the music would calm his fears. We were barely on the highway when Pete began to howl.

I figured Pete was singing and thought how cool it was that I had a music-loving doggie. I turned up the volume and serenaded with Pete. He howled even louder. It took me awhile to realize that Pete didn't like the music. Perhaps the sounds hurt his ears, I thought, as I turned off the radio. We drove the rest of the way in silence.

When I pulled into my driveway 3 hours later and opened the back door of the car, Pete bounded into my arms. How had he done that? He was firmly zippered in. I examined the fabric kennel and saw that he had chewed the zipper apart. Ripped it to shreds. Smart puppy. So much for the new crate. It went in the trash bin as I carried Pete into the house.

I put the puppy training pad in a strategic spot near the back door and set up his water bowl and food on the floor in the kitchen. Pete lapped up the water and explored the house. I'm pretty sure he even peed on the puppy pad for good measure. Good dog. Trained already.

I knew I was not going to allow Pete on the furniture or the bed. When he jumped up on the sofa, I gently moved him to the floor. He jumped back up. I put him down. Up and down. Up and down. We worked on that for quite a while until I gave up and let Pete cozy up to me on the sofa. He promptly fell asleep. So cute. Not trained.

Pete was still snoozing when it was bedtime. I turned out the lights and tiptoed out of the living room. When I reached the hallway, I looked around to see if he was still sleeping. Not so much. In fact, Pete was quietly tiptoeing behind me. Honest to goodness. It sure looked like a four-legged tiptoe.

I led Pete back to the living room and told him to lie in his bed. I fluffed it up and showed him that it was nice and cozy. Nope. Not going to happen. He just looked at me as if to say, "I'm going wherever you're going." My plan was to train him to sleep in his new bed, close to the puppy pads. He didn't seem to get it.

Not to be outwitted, I hurried to the bedroom and closed my door before he could enter. Pete whimpered. I got into bed. He cried louder, then began pawing the door frame. I tried to go to sleep, but there was so much scratching and crying, I knew I had better open the door.

After Pete saturated me with wet kisses, I got back into bed and told him to lie down on the carpet next to the bed. Pete jumped up to lie next to me. I got up and put him back on the floor. Up he jumped. I put him down. Up and down. Up and down. How was that little mite of a puppy able to easily spring to the bed? I gave up, and my second rule was broken. Not cute. Not trained.

Don't let your dog drink water from the toilet. I knew that would be an important training lesson. I'd faithfully put clean water in Pete's bowl every morning. It stayed full all day. I thought that was strange until I heard him lapping at the water in the toilet.

Thinking I should nip this in the bud, I closed the lid on the toilet. He found the other toilet. I closed that lid, too. I put fresh water in his bowl again and pointed to it on the floor. I might have even made lapping noises to show him how to drink. He stared at me, giving me "the look." I figured he'd drink it if he was thirsty.

Tired of that training strategy, I went to the living room and turned on the TV. Pete sat in front of me and continued his stare. He was definitely trying to tell me something, but I didn't yet know doggie talk. Later, when I was preparing for bed, I flushed the toilet. Pete bounded in and began taking long voracious laps.

Once again, I gave up my training regimen. Pete clearly expressed that he liked the cold water from the toilet. And he'd die of thirst before drinking from his clean bowl. From then on, I left the lid up. I made sure never to use that blue disinfectant that cleans when you flush, and I made sure to flush several times after I did clean the bowl. Not cute. Doggie not trained.

I had heard that using treats was a good way to train dogs. I was clever. I bought a box of little treats, morsels of tasty tidbits, and I would reward Pete for good behavior.

Pee on the bush outside. Good dog. Treat.

Poop in the yard. Good dog. Treat.

Within days, Pete was potty trained, and we no longer needed the puppy pads. Smart dog. Trained.

Pete had an affinity to dish towels and wash cloths. He thought it was fun to tease me with the towel hanging from the oven door. He'd return from the kitchen with the towel in his mouth and pace back and forth, never letting me actually grab the towel.

Again, I was clever. I'd lure him with a treat and we would trade. It worked well, until I realized that I was training him to get the towel for me. He got a treat every time he fetched the darn thing. Smart dog. Not so smart owner. Now I had to make sure that all towels and wash cloths were placed far back on the kitchen or bathroom counter.

I knew that I'd never, ever feed Pete from the table. We grew up with dogs and that was a rule in our home, even though we kids would slip food we didn't like to the floor, so the dog would eat it. I had already decided that I'd train Pete not to beg at the table. That didn't work so well, so I began to eat standing at the kitchen counter.

To this day, I eat my meals standing at the counter, unless I have company. Then we sit at the table. Regardless, Pete still begged, whether I was standing or sitting.

I'm not talking about the long, sad gaze kind of begging. I could ignore that. I'm talking about the whimpering and barking kind of begging. The "try to steal it off my plate" kind of begging. It was easier to just give the mutt a piece of meat or cheese. The darn dog even liked shrimp, though he'd pass up a green bean. I'll be the first to agree that I really messed up on that training endeavor.

When all is said and done, I did learn some important lessons of doggie ownership. Treats *do* help with training—if the tactic is done correctly. Pete was smart enough to know that I was like putty in his paws. He got to go out *and* get a treat if he stood by the back door, feigning the need for a potty break. He got to eat people food if he barked and howled loud enough. He got to sleep on the sofa and in my bed if he was persistent enough to get me tired of putting him back on the floor.

I figured I'd have to adjust my priorities or re-think my training routine. It wasn't working quite the way I had planned.

Rule #2:

Understand Traits of your Dog

Springer spaniels have an amazing leaping ability. Pete found that it was delightfully amusing to jump from the sofa to the recliner, a good four feet away, and back again. One evening, I was chatting on the phone with a friend and complained about all of the springing that Pete did.

"Duh," she said. "You got a *springer* spaniel."

How was I to know that a springer spaniel would spring? I just figured that some guy called Mr. Springer named the breed. After all, cocker spaniels don't cock.

Nonetheless, Pete was a springer. As a breed and as in him showing me what fun he could have on the furniture. No distance was too great, either in the house or outside. My boy could even leap *up* a five-foot rock wall. Effortlessly. I figured I'd best just get used to it. Can't change the stripes on a zebra.

I was a little worried about what to do about Pete when I had to return to school after summer vacation. Should I let him have the run of the house? Would I return to find the sofa in tatters? Pete had never chewed the furniture thus far, but would he panic if left alone for eight hours? What if he jumped up to the kitchen table or, worse, through a window pane to get out?

My sister, who's an experienced dog owner, suggested that I buy a metal kennel and crate Pete while I'm away. I could begin to get him accustomed to it before the school year began.

"I don't want to put him in a cage," I said. "He was born on a farm and likes his freedom."

My sister assured me that dogs want to have their own space, their own cave. "Put a towel over the top and blankets inside," she said. "You'll be surprised how often he'll just go in there to sleep."

I bought a nice, large kennel with plenty of room for Pete to move around. I made it warm and cozy and placed it next to the table where I did my schoolwork. Sure enough, Pete would go in of his own volition and snooze while I was working.

Did I mention that throwing a few treats in there was very enticing to him? Unfortunately, I was not allowed to close the door. He'd jump out as soon as I would try.

One day, not long after I had set up the crate, Pete was naughty. I can't remember what he did, but I decided that he needed a time out. I put him in the kennel and locked the door, sternly saying something like "Bad dog!" I went into the living room as Pete cried, yelped, barked, and howled. Nonstop.

After about 20 minutes, I couldn't take it any longer. I opened the kennel door and went to sit on the sofa—giving him the silent treatment. Pete hid under the coffee table. Never again would he go into the crate. Not even when I tossed in some treats. He was much happier when I moved it to the basement. Out of sight, out of mind.

I learned a few things from this experience. Pete *did* like a cave. As long as he didn't lose his freedom. He found his own personal space, and would snooze under a table, under a chair, or behind the recliner. And it had to be near me. If I changed my location, he followed me. Even into the bathroom.

This is a trait common to many dogs. They want to be with us and protect us. But I've learned that springers often bond with one person in the family. Pete never let me out of his sight. Ever. He probably felt very alone when I went to school. Nonetheless, he had the run of the house. No cage for my boy.

Pete had a very loud, high-pitched bark, especially when he was excited. Like when he'd find a squirrel or when we were playing frisbee. I figured his bark must be common to the breed since a springer needs to tell a hunter where to find the prey. I might have been wrong with my rationale, since Pete's bark could scare away anyone or anything in his path. I've since learned that not all springers have such an ear-piercing bark. Even his vet said it was unique.

Pete was very proud of his bark. He must have thought it made him sound manly. To me, it was like fingernails scraping a blackboard. I tried everything I could think of to stop Pete's loud bark, including barking back. I must have looked pretty ridiculous. Like a dog-trainer's nightmare. Several friends suggested those awful collars that shock the dog. I was tempted, I admit, but I couldn't do it. I wouldn't hurt Pete.

Don't get me wrong. Pete had another bark for less-exciting occasions. He also didn't bark constantly. Most of the day he snoozed on the sofa or he was lying quietly next to me. But when he did bark elatedly, it pierced my whole being. It was very annoying.

I remember one New Year's Day, when Pete was still a puppy. We'd had a few inches of snow that fell through the night, so I took Pete out to the yard and played snowball with him. Actually, I was trying to shovel the snow off the deck, and he was trying to catch the snow in his mouth. Pete absolutely loved our game and showed his delight by using his wildly excited bark.

For some reason, my usually quiet boy barked like a maniac when he was playing any kind of ball or if I was shoveling snow or raking leaves. I'm not sure if it was his way of saying "throw me the ball (snow), (leaves)," or if it was because of his exuberance that came from enjoying the game. It was a trait I was never able to train out of him.

Anyway, on that snowy morning, one of the neighbors yelled for us to be quiet. In not so nice terms. Did I mention it was about 8:30 a.m.? On New Year's Day?

I brought Pete in, but soon after got a visit from the dog warden. Yes, on New Year's Day. Luckily, we only got a warning about disturbing the peace. The neighbors must have had a late New Year's Eve, but I didn't think that was very kind.

Springers are hunting dogs. I planned *not* to train Pete as a hunter, but the trait is apparently inborn. After my dad passed away, Pete and I spent a lot of time at his place while we cleared out the house. Pete loved it there. I watched him turn into Mr. Macho Hunter Dog before my very eyes.

Ten acres, most of it as woods, is a springer's paradise. Pete could roam free, though he made sure I was sitting on the front porch before he investigated the area. He never seemed to wander too far. Nonetheless, I did train Pete to come home. I gave him a treat whenever he came back to the house, even if his exploration of the woods lasted only 3 minutes. "Good boy," I'd say. "You come home, you get a treat."

I started to notice that Pete would stop at a tree, sniff all around it and up the trunk, then stand very still with his tail wagging like crazy. If I didn't come see what he was showing me, he would begin barking that high-pitched bark.

I finally got it. Pete was telling me where a squirrel or a bird had been. He'd go from tree to tree doing the same thing. Pete only stopped barking if I said, "Good boy. Now find another one." Of course, the silence would be short-lived because he'd soon find the next tree that had been visited by any sort of wildlife.

Pete was in his glory. Me, not so much. After a while I'd say, "Enough animals. Let's go in." Pete would go right to the pantry. He comes home, he gets a treat. Smart dog.

During hunting season, Pete seemed to want to be out much longer. Usually he stayed near the house, always keeping it—and me—in his line of vision. Now he seemed to go deeper into the woods. He started bringing home his booty.

For three days in a row, Pete came to the front porch with a deer leg. Hoof and all. He'd have a big grin on his face and puff out his chest like he was king of the forest.

"Oh, my gosh," I'd say with disdain. "We have to put it in the trash." Pete got so annoyed with me for taking away his prize. He'd kind of stomp into the house like a petulant kid. Of course, stopping at the pantry for a treat.

Interestingly, Pete never brought home the fourth deer leg. Either he got smart and decided to hide it from me, or a coyote found it. Regardless, the hunter instinct is a part of this breed.

Numerous times, Pete would find an injured bird and bring it to me. I told someone how he would hold the bird in his mouth, but he was gentle with it and wanted me to have it. My friend who's a hunter said, "That's good. He's got a soft mouth and he's bringing you the prey."

A soft mouth, I learned, is a characteristic of this breed. It's an excellent trait if you get a springer for hunting or for being a family dog. In all his years, Pete never was a biter. Even if we were rough-housing and Pete grabbed my arm or hand with his mouth, he never bit down. His gentleness just came naturally.

Generally, springers have a nice disposition. And they're very social. Pete loved company and enjoyed being around people and other dogs. I've heard that inbreeding can result in a springer having bizarre personality traits but, thank goodness, that wasn't my experience. Even if I did something to annoy my boy, he got over it quickly.

Springers are intelligent, faithful, clever, personable, and gentle dogs. You might not even need treats to enhance training. Just persistence. You *will* need to work on the bark.

Rule #3:

Get Plenty of Exercise

I knew that springers are hunting dogs, so I figured Pete would need plenty of exercise. I bought a nice retractable leash and walked Pete faithfully when I got home from school and on weekends. We would no sooner return to the house before he'd be begging for another jaunt. I tired of the routine very quickly. Pete, not so much.

At the time, we lived two houses from the Lackawanna River in northeast Pennsylvania. The Lackawanna looks like a creek—unless we got a hurricane remnant or a nor'easter. Then it was a raging torrent. But I digress.

The family whose home was right on the river had three dogs. Maggie was a 15-year-old

Brittany spaniel with markings like Pete. Harvey was a chubby, older beagle, and Willie was some kind of short-legged, long haired shepherd dog.

Maggie took to Pete right away, acting like a surrogate mother. She'd groom Pete and nudge him to do appropriate doggie behavior. Pete was only about 6 weeks old when they met, and she continued the instruction that I'm sure Pete's own mother had started.

Harvey and Pete became the best of buddies. He would show Pete where to explore, and what to look for in the woods or by the river. Willie, on the other hand, pretty much did his own thing, and Pete never seemed to warm up to him. They just ignored each other.

Pete always wanted to visit with Maggie and Harvey. He'd dilly dally on our walk until Mr. Ross would come home and let out his dogs. Pete seemed to sense when his buddies could play, and he wasn't satisfied to sit at home without having had a chance to romp. So, Pete and I would walk up and down the street. Even in the winter. I got a lot of exercise. More than I wanted.

There was a steep bank to get to the river. I wasn't about to slide down on my fanny, but when Ross was out with his dogs, he'd tell me to let Pete off the leash. Pete and his buddies would follow Mr.

Ross down the hill to explore the land along the river.

During the summer, Mr. Ross would throw a stick in the river, and Maggie would jump in to fetch it. We watched Pete show the inner urging to follow her lead, but he was scared. He'd put a paw in the water, then jump back. Maggie would try to get Pete to follow her, but he just couldn't do it. He was such a wimp.

Harvey didn't like the water, and maybe he was saying, "Don't go there, bud." It took a little more encouragement from Maggie before Pete finally mustered his courage and went all in. Ross and I cheered; Pete grinned as he doggie paddled across the river. Then the games began. Ross would throw him a stick, and he'd hurry to swim out to get it. Maggie usually beat him to it, but that didn't deter Pete. He'd just retrieve the next one, happy as a lark.

Pete loved the water and was a natural swimmer. Once he was over his initial fear, he'd constantly beg to go swimming. As soon as I put on his leash and we exited the front door of the house, Pete took off toward the river, dragging me with him. Literally.

My sister chastised me when I told her about it. "Don't let him think he's the boss," she said. "Teach him how to heel." She explained that Pete should never be permitted to lead me. Instead, he should walk calmly by my side.

Pete and I practiced the routine over and over, up and down the street. "Walk nice," I'd say. "No, do it again. Walk nice." Pete seemed to catch on to the idea whenever we returned home, but he'd take off as soon as we were facing the river.

I always kept Pete on a short leash, using every muscle in my arms and legs to hold him at bay. He'd dig in his heals, lower his center of gravity, and pull me with all of his might toward the river. He looked like Spike the bulldog on Looney Tunes.

In time, I gave up. I'd just open the door and let him run, with me following behind with the leash. I knew exactly where he'd go, and I'd put him back on the leash when I got to the river. The funny thing was, Pete knew what he was doing. He'd wear me down until he got his way. In reality, he could heel if he wanted to.

Remember the dog warden on New Year's Day? As the kind man was leaving, he stood with the front door open. Before I could say a word of warning, Pete bounded between the warden's legs and bolted toward the river. The warden apologized profusely, saying he knew better than to talk by an open door. He ran after Pete with his rope, catching him at the river's edge. Pete gave his quirky grin, then walked back home side by side with the warden as if he were the lead contender at the Westminster dog show.

Unfortunately, new neighbors moved across the street from Ross's house. They told us very clearly that they would call the police if any of the dogs were off leash. Pete's swimming and running days were over. It was a sad day for all of us.

I fenced our back yard, so Pete could get the exercise he needed, then installed a doggie door in the kitchen. "Look Pete," I showed him. "You can go in and out whenever you want."

Pete stared at the flap in the door but wasn't about to try it. He was always timid until he got the hang of something. It wasn't until Harvey came for a play date, and had great fun going in and out of the house, that Pete finally followed suit. In fact, I could imagine Harvey saying, "You're lucky, dude. Wish I had one of these." Once Harvey gave his approval, Pete took ownership.

The yard became Pete's domain. I hung a bird feeder under the deck so that Pete could watch for birds. He never went after them but reveled in the occasional feathers he found in the yard. He would jump up and down, a kind of happy dance, picking up the feather to toss in the air. Pete particularly liked big, black crow feathers. At least I assumed they were crow feathers. Maybe they were hawk feathers. Anyway, they were more fun than any toy for Pete. And he got plenty of exercise.

Pete taught me a lot about the need for exercise, even as we both aged. In our younger years, we both had plenty of pent-up energy. Pete snoozed all through the day while I was at work. At least, that's what I assumed, though I found remains of doggie slobber on the den window. By the time I got home, he wanted to run and play. I wanted to sit on the sofa.

If I had my way, we both would have become sluggish and lethargic. Lazy, for sure.

I learned from Pete that exercise is any kind of joyful activity that moves the body and refreshes the soul. A walk wasn't just a routine to burn calories. It was an adventure of finding the perfect stick to carry home or discovering the scenic route for trail marking. For me, it was a time of seeing the beauty of nature, watching doggies at play, and noticing how animals communicate with each other.

Pete was a sociable and well-behaved boy because of the exercise he got. And I reaped the benefits by not having to worry about a destructive pet. The icing on the cake is that I was happy and peace-filled myself.

Rule #4:

Socialize Your Dog

Pete enjoyed all of the socialization he got with Maggie, Harvey, and Willie. Well, not so much Willy. For some reason, Pete never seemed to take to him. I suppose it's like when we meet a person and there's just no connection.

Even though Ross would bring Harvey to play with Pete in our yard, Harvey eventually wearied of the outing and just wanted to snooze. He was getting old, and no longer fancied exploring. Maggie, too, was up in age. And Pete began to think of her in terms other than motherly, if you get my drift. Maggie clearly told Pete that there was to be no funny business. Their friendship could only be platonic.

When the visits with Harvey ended, Pete needed new companionship. He took to sunning himself on the deck in late afternoon, waiting for the school bus to return with the little boy who lived down the block. Pete would call out with that high-pitched bark for Damien to come and play with him. Over the years, they became best friends.

One time, Damien asked if he could take Pete for a walk. We got out the leash and I warned Damien to hold Pete tightly because he tended to run to the river. We were no sooner out the front door when Pete took off. Unfortunately, Damien was no match for Pete's gait, and the boy went flying through the air like Superman until Pete stopped suddenly. Probably to pee on the fire hydrant. Damien crashed to the ground, still holding the leash. I ran to see if he was OK.

"Why didn't you let go?" I asked.

"You said to hold on tight," he replied with a quirky grin.

Luckily, Damien wasn't hurt, but we decided it was safer to curtail the walks. He and Pete could play in the yard.

The neighbor whose front yard abutted my fence had a German shepherd/lab mix dog named Goliath. Goliath was an unfixed male, as was Pete. If he came near the fence, Pete barked ferociously. So annoying.

Interestingly, Goliath never barked back, but he would pee by the fence. Of course, Pete would pee at the same spot on the other side, marking his territory. Goliath would find another location along the fence line, and Pete would follow suit. In time, we had no grass on either side which was quite handy because we didn't need to use a weed whacker there when we mowed our lawns.

At first, I thought that Pete's barking was a warning to Goliath. Then I noticed that it was the same high pitch as when he'd call to Damien. I suggested to my neighbor that we could let Goliath into the yard to see if the dogs would play nice together. He agreed.

As soon as I opened the gate, Pete stopped barking and looked warily at Goliath. Goliath looked at Pete. Pete sniffed all over Goliath's body. Goliath did the same. They began to lick each other, especially aiming for private parts. Their friendship was forged.

Every day, Pete seemed to know when it was time for Mr. Charlie, our neighbor, to come home from work. Even if Pete had been snoozing under the kitchen table or playing with Damien, he'd use the doggie door and lie on the deck as 5 p.m. approached. As soon as Charlie pulled into his driveway, Pete would bark excitedly until Goliath came bounding to our yard. That would be my signal to open the gate, unless Damien was there to do it, and the two doggie buddies would chase each other around the yard.

One afternoon, early in the friendship stage, I was sitting at the table on my deck, and Goliath came up the steps to check me out. As he began sniffing me, Pete growled, then went into attack mode. Clearly, Pete was my protector and he wasn't about to let Goliath get close to me.

Pete lunged at Goliath. Before I knew it, there was a full-blown war. The table was over-turned, and the deck umbrella went flying. Both fully engaged in the fracas, Goliath clamped onto Pete's muzzle as I tried to pry the two dogs apart.

Charlie came running and took Goliath home. We both checked our dogs for injuries. Goliath was fine, but Pete had a small gash on his cheek. Goliath won the battle, or so I had thought.

I learned several things following that incident. First, even though Pete acted like a wimp in most situations, he had bonded with me and would never let anyone, or anything, hurt me. I had not one iota of concern about what I would do if a burglar tried to break into my home. Soft-hearted

Pete would take a bullet before he'd let anyone near me.

Second, unfixed male dogs are alpha dogs. Each wants to be the boss. I figured that if Goliath's owners would ever let him come back, the dogs couldn't be left alone in the yard.

Third, and a most interesting discovery, battles between alpha dogs establish clear boundaries, but engender no grudges. Pete begged for Goliath to come into the yard the next afternoon when Charlie arrived home. Goliath sat at the gate, waiting for me to open it.

Charlie and I looked at each other, wondering what to do. We finally agreed to let the dogs play, but we both kept close watch to assure that neither dog would initiate a fight.

Pete and Goliath frolicked as if nothing had happened the day before. In fact, Pete began to hump Goliath—and Goliath let him. Pete was not a humper, so this seemed like a strange development to me. I mentioned it to Pete's vet, who explained that such behavior was not sexual. It just indicated that Goliath recognized Pete as the boss.

Pete and Goliath developed a deep and loving friendship. They played together every day, for nearly five years, regardless of the weather conditions. Neither rain nor snow would keep them apart. Goliath's owner told me that when Pete and I moved, Goliath would just sit by the fence and wait for Pete to come out and play. He didn't seem to understand that Pete wasn't coming back.

During the same time period, Mr. Ross asked if I would take in a rescue dog whose owner could no longer care for him. I reluctantly agreed to accept the Jack Russel terrier on a trial basis, thinking that Pete might want company when I was at school. I named him Jack. I know that wasn't very creative, but I wasn't sure that the deal would work out.

Jack made himself at home right away. He took over Pete's toys, and would eat Pete's food. Pete wasn't happy about it, but that little terrier was a terror. He made it perfectly clear that he was boss. Why Pete didn't stand up for his rights, I don't know.

When it was time for bed on Jack's first night in our home, Jack jumped up on the bed and wouldn't allow Pete to do so. I put Jack on the floor and told Pete to claim his spot. Instead, Jack jumped back up and growled ferociously at Pete. Pete spent the night on the floor. He was not a happy boy.

The next day, Pete tried to reclaim his space to no avail. Pete didn't fight; he didn't bark. He surrendered. That little terror—I mean terrier— allowed him nothing.

By the third day, Pete hid in the corner behind a living room chair and stopped eating. I didn't like Jack. I didn't like that he sat next to me on the sofa and claimed the other half of my bed. I wanted my Pete.

On the fifth day, I returned Jack to his owner. After that experience, I used to tell Pete he was a lucky boy. We had been pals for a long time; Jack lasted only five days. I think Pete knew what I was talking about. And I believe it was a lesson for both of us.

I learned that Pete didn't want to share his space with another dog. He liked his playtime with friends, but when he was done, it was just Pete and me. He liked that.

For me, I realized that Pete was indeed special. We were like two peas in a pod. He knew what I was thinking; he sensed my emotions. We had a special bond. I didn't feel the same way about Jack. I knew I'd never warm up to him, even if he hadn't been so nasty to Pete.

I had no connection with Jack. I guess you know innately when you've found the right dog. Pick one you can live with. If not, it'll be a long 12-15 years or more. Maybe that's why there are so many doggies looking for a forever home.

After we moved, Pete never again had a friend quite like Goliath, Harvey, or Maggie. He never forgot his buddies, either. Occasionally Pete and I would sit on the sofa and talk about each of them. His tail would wag at the mention of one of their names, then he'd throw back his head and give a long, baying wail. I called it Pete's sad song, knowing he missed his playmates terribly. Now that Pete's gone, I know how he felt. Makes me want to sing a sad song myself, just thinking about it.

Pete did make an acquaintance with a neighbor's dog when we stayed at Dad's house on the hill. She was a pit-bull mix, very calm, named Kayla. When the neighbors took their daily walks with Kayla, she always stopped by to visit with Pete. But it had to be on her terms. No funny business, no sniffing in private body places. "Just stopping by to say howdy," it seemed like Kayla said to Pete. Then she'd be on her way.

It didn't work the other way around. If Pete took a walk to her house, it looked like he was either ignored or told in doggie talk to take his leave. Kayla must have been emphatic in a quiet way. Pete would just tuck his little nub of a tail between his legs and head on home.

From then on, or maybe just because he was getting old, Pete seemed to lack an interest in having new doggie friends. He made up for it by making people friends.

As soon as he alerted me that a neighbor or acquaintance was arriving, he stood at the door waiting for their visit. Not so patiently. "Hurry to see me," he'd call in that high-pitched bark like he had used to invite Damien or Goliath to play. It was an added bonus if my friends brought a treat for Pete.

As soon as a visitor sat on the sofa, Pete sprung up next to our guest, somehow easing himself under an arm or on a lap. Then he'd roll on his back and insist on belly rubs, quite comfy and hospitable. This was no easy feat or light burden. By then, Pete weighed about 55 pounds. Nonetheless, he seemed to think that our company had come to see him. Luckily, my friends obliged.

Pete taught me the importance of friends. He showed me that we can miss the ones we love, but they will always remain in our hearts. I was a failure at so many training attempts, but I made sure to instill a sense of hospitality, of being social, in Pete. We liked our quiet time together, but we enjoyed our visitors as well. It was one of Pete's traits that will always engender in me very happy memories.

Rule #5:
Recognize Your Dog's Personality

Personality encompasses the numerous traits that define all of us. Animals are no different. Some qualities that dogs possess may be inherent in the breed. Others may just be a component of a dog's temperament. One of the things I found so endearing about Pete was his sensitive nature. He recognized when I was happy or sad, and he knew when I needed a cuddle or when he should give me some space.

Someone once told me that dogs don't have emotions, but I disagree. I could see when Pete was sad, and he literally smiled when he was happy. He could be grumpy, and he could be petulant. If he was upset, he'd hide behind a chair and lick his paws.

Not only was Pete sensitive to my feelings, but he also understood the English language. He'd react to whatever I said. Sometimes I had to spell words so as not to trigger a response from Pete if I was talking on the phone to a friend.

One of my brothers scoffed when I told him that Pete understood English. Tom's not a dog lover and can't understand why anyone would want an animal in the house. I'm not sure how that happened because he grew up with dogs.

Anyway, my brother argued that dogs only understand the tone of your voice, not the meaning of the words. "Not true," I disagreed. "I'll show you."

"Pete, let's go to the basement." Without any clue from me, Pete went to the basement door. In the same tone, I said, "Pete, help me get something in the garage." Pete went to the garage door. Finally, I said, "Pete, go look out the window." Pete jumped up on the recliner and looked out the window. I thought my argument was pretty convincing.

Not only did Pete understand what I was saying, he had a way of speaking to me. I began to see that he responded to my questions by rapidly wagging his tail. For example, I could say, "Do you want to go out?" If he wagged his tail very quickly, that meant *yes*. No tail wagging meant *no*.

Most people were skeptical when I told them about Pete answering my questions. After all, of course his tail would wag on an invitation to go out. But ask him if he wanted his ear medicine. Believe me, there was no tail wagging.

I don't think this is a trait of all breeds, but I think it may be part of a springer spaniel. In fact, many members of the springer Facebook group call it "wiggle butt." All dogs wag their tails, but not like the rapid flapping of a springer. It's incredibly cute and definitely meant as communication. Pete's tail wagged very quickly when he stood by a tree to say, "Yes, the squirrel just went up a tree." He might have sniffed another tree, but if his tail didn't wag, I'd recognize that there had been no squirrel on that one.

Another personality trait that I noticed in Pete was that he wasn't very comfortable in new situations. Don't get me wrong. Pete was very sociable and liked to be around people and other animals. Except cats. Pete was petrified of cats— even little kittens. I don't know why, unless he had a bad experience with kitties at the farm where he was born.

There were a lot of feral cats living near the river by our home in Archbald. They would prance by our fenced yard, seeming to say to Pete, "Ha!

You're stuck in there and we can roam around in freedom."

Pete would go ballistic. He'd run back and forth along the fence line, barking up a storm. That seemed to enhance the cats' enjoyment of teasing him.

I tried to desensitize Pete by introducing him to kittens. We went to the pet store and visited the cat section. Now the tide was changed, and the kitties were the ones in cages. That was fine by Pete. Pete would slowly investigate, doing a little sniffing. The cat would hiss. Pete would go ballistic.

I'd deliberately walk Pete to the feral cats' hideaway near the river, and he'd tentatively explore the surroundings. He knew there were kitties nearby, long before I did. As soon as we got close to their habitat, even I could hear the hiss. Pete would bark hysterically, then run—pulling me along with him.

We visited my uncle who had an older, more sedate feline. Though the cat was snoozing on the cushion of a chair, he opened one eye as we approached and hissed his warning. Again, Pete went ballistic.

Likewise, my niece came to visit and brought her cat, Molly. Even Molly hissed if Pete merely looked in her direction.

I'm not sure why every cat hissed at Pete when he came close. In every case, from my perspective, Pete approached quietly, merely showing curiosity. Perhaps in the animal world, Pete emitted a smell of fear, a scent of impending danger. Regardless, every hiss was a reinforcement to him that felines were the enemy.

One night when my niece was staying with me, I was getting into bed and Pete began barking hysterically. I told him that he was acting crazy. Molly was in the basement. Pete kept looking under the bed, still barking. My niece came in to check on the ruckus. Sure enough, Pete was correct. Molly was hiding in the box spring batting. I gave up on the desensitizing. Might as well accept that Pete didn't like cats.

Girl doggies were a different story. Pete liked the pretty girls. Even the not so pretty ones. I guess that's true of all boy doggies. As you know, once Pete got out of the puppy stage, even his surrogate mother avoided him. Maggie recognized that Pete was a lecher. Still, some girls didn't care. They thought Pete was cute.

When our neighbor's mother stopped by our home by the river, she'd let her little white poodle come visit—on the other side of the fence. Pete was a happy boy and would have enjoyed a fun romp in the grass. That little sweetheart of a dog acted coquettish and coy, toying with Pete's affections.

On the other hand, remember Kayla, the pit bull mix belonging to the neighbors near my dad's house? Kayla needed no fence for protection. She'd come to visit Pete every day, but if he came too close, she had a very convincing growl that would warn him to keep his distance. Some girls are like that.

As you know, Pete also liked boys. It didn't matter what kind. Little boys like Damien or boy doggies like Goliath and Harvey. Pete seemed to take to them right away, no matter their size or shape. Maybe it was just a guy thing, but I accepted it as part of Pete's personality.

Pete liked other types of animals, as well, but they were more in the realm of hunting. At least that's how I perceived his fascination with them. Pete particularly liked the cute little chipmunks that lived in the rock wall below dad's front yard. They seemed to enjoy teasing Pete, often emerging from their crevices to lead Pete on a chase, only to disappear into another cranny. Surprisingly, Pete never barked at them. In fact, he liked the game, and they became his friends.

Pete wasn't comfortable with anything that made a lot of racket. I should have remembered that from my first ride in the car with Pete when he howled at the radio. But I didn't.

A few of my friends suggested that I turn on the TV to keep Pete company through the day when I was at school. Some even noted that their pets liked watching animal shows. I found a channel featuring dogs, even pointing to them on the screen. Pete showed no interest. He wouldn't even look at the TV. In fact, he made it clear that he wanted no noise while I was gone.

Noise was Pete's nemesis. One of my brothers suggested that I bang a few pots and pans if I was trying to teach Pete not to do something. I did that once when he was a puppy, but he cowered in fear and hid under the coffee table. I learned my lesson. Pete hated noise of any kind. In fact, I didn't need to raise my voice with Pete. Ever. Pointing a finger with a stern look had Pete apologizing for any misdemeanor. He said he was sorry by rapidly wagging his tail.

It was frustrating to try to vacuum the carpet. Anything with a motor was very scary to Pete. In addition to vacuum cleaners, lawn mowers, hair dryers, and weed whackers all elicited wild barking. Did I mention his very annoying bark?

No amount of acclimation ever calmed Pete's fears about machinery. He would bark if I even took the vacuum out of the closet. I bought a Roomba, figuring it didn't look like a vacuum. But I couldn't fool my boy. The Roomba's even scarier. It moves around the room all by itself. And it sounds like a vacuum.

I suppose I can understand that the noise from a motor can cause fear in a dog, but we had a similar problem whenever something beeped loudly. I had to go out and buy a timer with a single chirp because the oven timer would buzz until I turned it off. Pete would bark continuously. Same when the battery died on the smoke detectors.

One night, the detector went off in the bedroom. Pete went ballistic. As hard as I tried, I couldn't get the battery out of the contraption to replace it. I finally gave up and went back to bed. Between the constant beeping and Pete's barking, there was no sleep for either of us that night.

Another personality trait that Pete possessed was his desire to be the boss in our home. It might have been a vestige of his male assertiveness, his instinct to be the alpha dog of our little pack, but I knew not to surrender my leadership. Pete tried often to usurp his power. When he didn't get his way, Pete would sulk.

I'd like to believe that I trained Pete to know that he needed to be submissive to me. In some way, the clang of the pots and the punishment in the wire kennel when he was a puppy might have served to elevate my status. Somewhat like Pete's attack on Goliath to show who's in charge. Whatever my inadvertent training tactic had been, it worked.

The other technique I used to emphasize my dominance was the silent treatment. Pete hated that one. I'd cross my arms and turn my back on Pete. When he'd stomp around to face me, I'd turn the other way. I didn't have to say a word. It might have been a *Dog Whisperer* trick that I picked up from watching the videos, and it was very effective. Once Pete was in the submissive position, I'd quietly say, "You're not the boss. I'm the boss." Pete's tail would wag in agreement.

I imagine male dogs will often try to regain their alpha status, and Pete was no different. He would test his boundaries occasionally, but not often. On the other hand, I did give Pete some responsibilities, so he could maintain his dignity. It was his job to protect me, and I told him so. "You take care of me," I'd say, "And I take care of you."

My sensitive and protective mutt didn't like me to use ladders or step stools. Neither make any noise, but they're scary. I figured Pete's bark was warning me that I could fall, even if I was only using the first few rungs. He'd bark if I was hanging a picture on the wall, changing the batteries in the smoke detectors, or replacing light bulbs in ceiling fixtures.

As crazy as it sounds, I kept the clock on the living room wall set to standard time, even when we were in daylight savings time. It was easier for me to make the time conversion than to get out the ladder and put up with all the commotion.

Pete did teach me a thing or two while he shared his likes and dislikes. Getting up on a ladder when you've reached an age that makes it precarious is not wise. And is it really necessary to weed whack? Pulling the weeds is much more cathartic, and the results last longer. I'd have given up the vacuum, too, but no one told me that springers shed. A lot.

I think it's important to understand your dog's innate personality. It helps to build the on-going relationship that will engender healthy cohabitation. If you learn your pet's temperament, you'll know what triggers might lead to behavior problems. And I feel certain that our dogs are sizing up our personalities, as well. Pete recognized when he could take an inch and when to back off. He knew what brought me contentment and what made me upset. He taught me that life was pleasant when we understood each other. We made a good pair.

Rule #6:
Springers Need Grooming

I have to admit, I didn't like brushing my dog or looking for ticks on him. I didn't like worrying that Pete could carry fleas into the house. And I really didn't like cleaning his ears. Pete wasn't crazy about those things either. Each of them was an essential task, but I preferred to pay someone else to take care of it. And it didn't come cheap.

Springers have a remarkable coat of fur. When Pete was a puppy, he had short hair, close to the skin. I was amazed when Pete's hair began to grow on the back of his arms and legs. It's called feathering. He also developed a mane, of which he was very proud. Believe it or not, I didn't realize that Pete would become a hairy boy.

I made the mistake of telling Pete's first groomer to cut it all off, because he was shedding all over the place. Pete was not happy, and he told me so. He was grumpy about it for days. I eventually learned to go easy on the cut, leaving his mane and feathering intact, but trimmed. We'd go a little shorter on the feathering because it got easily matted if he had been romping in the grass. Mulch from the gardens was always getting tracked into the house.

Pete worked hard at keeping himself cleaned up. His mother taught him well. He stayed busy licking his arms, his mane, and his privates. Obviously, there were places he couldn't reach, but dirt surprisingly fell off him. Pete could have been a muddy mess after a walk on a rainy day, but when he dried, the dirt disappeared. Of course, it had fallen to my floor or sofa, but with a nice neutral décor, it didn't show. Much. Besides, it got covered with a layer of hair.

As Pete aged, he didn't like to get dirty. I guess it was too much work to do all that licking to keep himself groomed. He began to refuse to go out in the rain, and he'd only walk on wet grass if it was an emergency.

On the other hand, Pete loved to roll in deer poop, even when he was older. What is it about specific types of excrement that attracts dogs? Deer and duck poop were Pete's favorites. Oh, my! He was as proud as a peacock when he'd rubbed that green goo all over his back and ears.

I used to try to squirt him with a hose or wipe it off with paper towels, despite his protests that I was ruining his life. The darn stuff was really hard to remove. As with so many other things, I finally stopped fighting about it. It eventually dried and fell off onto my rugs and sofa. But it didn't show. I used a lot of Febreze.

Ticks were gross. I'd had them pretty well controlled with monthly applications of Frontline. Once we moved to a condo and Pete wasn't foraging in the woods, I figured there wouldn't be a problem with ticks any longer. Wrong. I still constantly picked them off him. It was worse when I'd find them on an ear. Pete hated me to touch his ears, and those critters were difficult to grab on such a sensitive spot. I learned my lesson. Don't stop the tick and flea treatments. Ever.

Trips to the groomer are essential, unless you plan to spend lots of time grooming your springer. As I mentioned, the feathering on limbs and chest can get long and it's easily matted. Hair between toes can be annoying to a hairy dog, and tangles under the ears can lead to ear infections which are quite common in a springer.

Experienced groomers often ask if you want a springer cut or a field cut. I didn't know the difference, though I soon learned that the springer cut is more expensive. Get the field cut unless you plan to enter your dog in competitions.

Our first groomer wasn't too experienced with the breed. I told her to cut off all his hair, so he wouldn't be too hot in the summer. She shaved him, even on his backside. Pete hated it. He walked around like he was trying to cross his back legs, seeming to know that his privates were getting too much air. Even Damien remarked, "Wow. Pete's got big kahoonies." I had no idea how to respond.

Pete was itchy all over after his shave, so I began to use some medicated powder to soothe the irritation. He liked that. From then on, whenever Pete was doing a lot of licking "down there," I'd ask him if he wanted some powder. If he wagged his tail quickly, I knew it meant *yes*. He'd jump up on the bed and roll over on his back, spreading his legs, so I could sprinkle where he wanted it. Very strange, I know, but it worked for us.

We typically only went to the groomers twice a year, in the spring and late summer. During the winter, I'd usually trim the back of Pete's arms and legs and cut out the mats under his floppy ears. I finally found a groomer who knew that Pete wasn't a show dog, and she explained that I wanted more of a field cut. She was also experienced enough to know that a springer is very proud of the chest mane. She'd trim it appropriately but left it fluffy. Pete was happy with the results. I know because he told me so.

I'm not sure why I found grooming Pete to be such an unpleasant task. I had bought all kinds of tools and brushes. Even electric clippers. Of course, clippers didn't set well with Pete. The buzz of the motor had him running for cover. So, I got a hand-held shave thing. He didn't like that either.

Toenails were just about impossible for me to trim. I had read that you have to be very careful not to clip too close to the quick, so Pete might have sensed my nervousness. He'd howl and cry if I just positioned the toenail clippers near his paw.

As you know, Pete's ears were particularly sensitive. I'd try to wash the underside and into the ear canal, practically lying on Pete to keep him still. As soon as he could squirm out of my grasp, he'd hide behind the recliner.

Patience is not one of my virtues so, like so many other training issues, I just gave up. The groomer is experienced and has the equipment to hold the dog in place. Of course, the groomer also has wire kennels to shelter the dogs until their owners return. Not good, from Pete's perspective.

Pete didn't like visits to the groomer. He did look forward to a ride in the car, but as soon as we'd pull into the parking lot and he realized where we were, he'd cry and howl. I'd drag him in—literally. And he'd still be crying and howling when I returned for him.

Other dogs didn't seem to react like Pete did at the groomers. They waited patiently for their turn and relished the pampering. Not my sensitive mutt. I tried to explain to Pete that not everything in life is pleasant. Sometimes we just have to do what we've got to do. He didn't care, Pete told me. He'd rather be dirty and hairy. I preferred not to compromise on that one.

Rule #7:
Keep Your Dog Healthy

I had sticker shock after my first visit to the vet. When I told my dad the cost, he reminded me that "a fool and his money soon part." I also got the lecture about Dad's dog when he was a boy. His mutt never needed vet care. Yeah, right. The dog wasn't even allowed in the house, except in the dead of winter—and then it was relegated to the unheated basement.

It wasn't worth an argument. That's how it was in the old days. I also knew darn well that Dad didn't stick to those rules with our family dogs when I was a kid. Still, I was judicious about using the vet when Pete was a puppy. We went only when important vaccines were required. All in all, he had been pretty healthy in his youth.

Ear problems were the most common of Pete's issues. Because they were prone to infection, it was important to clean inside his ears regularly. Usually yeast was the culprit. It made sense since it was dark and moist under those floppy ears. The vet prescribed ear drops that would keep the yeast under control.

Believe me, I tried to keep up with the protocol. Pete ran when I got out the ear medicine. Even when I was persistent, Pete was quite adept at turning to the opposite direction each time I'd try to lift an ear. In fact, it was almost impossible to try to hold Pete's head and put drops in the canal.

And of course, Pete barked incessantly as if he was being tortured. I decided to let the vet take care of his ears. Pete was a little more acquiescent if the doctor did it. Yes, I know. A fool and his money soon part. Looking back, I do wish I had invested in pet insurance when Pete was a puppy. Naïvely, I thought the only time we'd need to see the vet was when he needed vaccines. Such was not the case.

Pete's health took a turn for the worse when my dad had a stroke. Pete was about 8 years old. He and I were traveling back and forth from my home to dad's house, and I was spending a lot of time with dad in rehab. Pete didn't like being left alone so often, and I was preoccupied with dad's care while trying to keep up with my schoolwork.

I noticed that Pete was taking a long time to pee on every bush when we'd go outside. In fact, he was peeing a lot, then he'd come in and drink down all of the water in the toilet. I was a little worried that he was drinking too much but didn't have time to deal with it. Pete ate well and didn't seem sick. As time went on, he seemed happy to hunt for animals, and I figured he needed to have a lot of pee for marking all the bushes in the woods. I was wrong.

After a second massive stroke, dad said he wanted to come home to die. We put a hospital bed in the family room and hired round-the-clock aides. Between hospice staff, nurses, and the many family and friends who came to visit during dad's last days, I was amazed at how accepting Pete was to the variety of people, many of whom he didn't know. He didn't bark, nor did he get much attention. He did seem to like the fact that we were mainly ordering pizza or sandwiches for our meals, and he made sure to be around the table begging for food.

The week after dad's funeral, all the people went home. It was back to just Pete and me. I wasn't paying him much attention, until I heard him retching in the family room. When I got there, I found a huge pile of black tarry mess on the carpet.

I had no idea what it was, but websites I checked indicated a very serious condition of stomach bleeding. Every internet source said to get the dog to emergency care right away.

It was a Friday night after 11 p.m., and I was three hours away from Pete's vet. I decided to watch and wait. The next morning, Pete was throwing up massive amounts of red blood. This was terribly bad, no doubt about it. I googled to find a local animal hospital, and the staff told me to bring him immediately.

The vet said that Pete was extremely sick and horribly dehydrated. He needed intravenous fluids and electrolytes, recommending that Pete be admitted to the hospital right away. She also wanted to do bloodwork. I asked her to check him for diabetes.

"What would make you associate his throwing up blood with diabetes?" she asked. I told her how much he had been drinking and peeing. Sure enough, Pete's blood sugar was sky high. She started him on insulin right away.

Pete was in the hospital for three days while they worked on nursing him back to health. The vet told me she wasn't sure if Pete would make it. Besides grieving for my father, I was beside myself with worry about my boy. There was no way I could handle another death in the same week. We were both ecstatic when Pete was finally allowed to come home.

We never found the actual cause of Pete's stomach bleeding, although an ulcer was suspected. The diabetes, the vet said, could have been genetic or it may have been triggered by all the stress of the previous few months. She didn't know if Pete's diabetes would be transient. That after his stomach healed, Pete's pancreas would go back to producing insulin. Unfortunately, it didn't. His diabetes was permanent.

Pete's new vet wanted him on a special diet of home-cooked chicken and rice. She taught me how to administer the insulin and test his urine for glucose and ketones. She also told me to text her Pete's glucose levels every morning and evening, and she would text back how many units of insulin to inject. She was amazing, and I'll never forget her kindness. Still, I was overwhelmed.

I began reading labels on dog food and treats. I was astonished to discover that Pete's favorite kibbles were loaded with high fructose corn syrup, as were his treats. I'm not talking about only one brand. Just about every single kind of dog treat has sugar. No wonder he loved them so much.

After months of preparing real chicken and rice after Pete's hospitalization, I switched to a chicken and rice formula kibble that had no sugar or corn syrup. Pete liked that I would mix in about ½ cup of baked chicken. I bought a lot of chicken. Good thing Pete was a bird dog.

I can't lie. This time was extremely stressful for Pete and me. Our entire routine changed, our eating patterns changed, and we were not in our home environment. I felt the need to be close to the wonderful vet who gave me the support I needed to manage Pete's diabetes. And, as dad's executor, I had to begin the process of closing his estate. It made sense for me to put my home in Archbald on the market and live in dad's house until I found my own place.

Pete and I did the best we could. The first challenge was to check his urine glucose twice a day. Pete wasn't used to having me follow him around with a Dixie cup. In the morning, he'd stop peeing as soon as he'd sense my presence, then run to a far-away bush and let it all out. By afternoon, having had the run of 10 acres, he refused to pee for me. We eventually worked it out by my putting Pete on the leash in dad's yard every morning and taking him on-leash to the local park in the afternoons. Once I got the cup filled, I'd carefully transport it back to the house to use the test strip.

The urine check wasn't as accurate as testing Pete's blood, but it gave me an indication of his glucose levels before breakfast and supper. Based on the results, I knew how many units of insulin to administer. Getting Pete to sit still for his twice-a-day injections after his meals was also not easy. I'd put two small sugar-free treats in my pocket and have him get up on a chair to look out the window. It took me awhile to get the knack of it, but I could eventually get that needle in and out before Pete begged for the treats he knew I had waiting for him.

The other problem was Pete's stomach. He threw up at least once every two weeks or so. Usually immediately after he ate. We didn't know the cause, although he had been diagnosed with a malignant mast cell tumor that had been biopsied and removed about two years prior. The vet said it wouldn't be unusual for it to metastasize to the digestive tract. I didn't plan to put Pete through chemotherapy, so I was hoping the stomach upset was just from stress. He was a sensitive boy and worried about everything.

Diabetes is difficult to manage in people, and even more challenging to handle in animals. Too much insulin or not enough insulin can both result in death. The reality of that weighed heavily on me. It may have figured into my decision to purchase a condo with just a patio, not a yard. A smaller, contained enclosure made our rituals much easier. I became very adept at reaching the Dixie cup under Pete to collect the pee every morning and afternoon, no longer needing the leash. Pete also knew the routine and was very obliging.

In time, settled into our new home, Pete and I had accepted the new reality. His blood sugar was relatively stable, needing only minor adjustments to the dose of insulin, so I tested his urine only in the mornings. Except for stomach upsets, Pete seemed to be doing fine. But I knew I couldn't let down my guard. Lucky for us, Pete had only one diabetic crash in the three years following his diagnosis, but it was so frightening that I never wanted to experience another.

I had just given Pete his insulin when he threw up all his food. I had figured he would beg for treats after his stomach settled, but he didn't. He fell asleep and didn't even want to go out before bedtime. I awoke in the middle of the night to hear Pete whimpering. Groggily, I called for him to come up on the bed, but he cried even more. When I turned on the light, Pete was in a total seizure. I knew immediately that he needed food, but he couldn't even stand. I dragged him to the kitchen and searched for anything I thought he would eat—cheese, treats, kibbles. Pete soon stopped shaking but was walking around in a daze. You want to know the weird thing? I never thought to give him sugar. That would have brought him out of it immediately. From then on, I waited at least half an hour after he had eaten before giving the boy his insulin shot. Live and learn.

As a dietitian, I knew that excess insulin makes a person ravenously hungry. It had the same reaction in Pete. He begged for food constantly, foraging for any crumb or morsel he could find. I was forced to seriously curtail snacking, which wasn't a bad thing, but it was a pain in the neck. My friend, who watched Pete when I was having surgery, told me she used to go out to eat in her car when she got hungry.

Eventually, Pete developed a food allergy. The vet suspected that the chicken and rice diet was the culprit, but it could also have been a gluten intolerance triggered by Pete's dog food or treats. I read every label and tried every brand of specialty formulas. None of them eliminated the itchy, runny eyes and nose that became a source of irritation for Pete. Pete's nose became cracked and dry, even bleeding at times.

The vet prescribed special eye drops and cream, all of them expensive though not especially effective. They were soothing, I suppose, because sometimes Pete would sit and stare at me as if he were asking for something. I'd say, "Do you want drops in your eyes?" He'd wag his tail.

Pete taught me that aging comes with a variety of ailments that can be overwhelming. Sometimes illness is beyond our control. Best thing to do is try to stay healthy. It's no different with our pets. It's just harder to figure out what they need.

I had read that dogs could be given Benadryl for their allergies. The whole tablet made Pete too groggy, so I began to cut them in half. Getting him to actually ingest the pill was another story. Even when I'd hide it in a piece of cheese or chicken, I'd find the little pink nub on the kitchen floor. Trying to outsmart my boy, I'd then hide the medicine-encased meat in his bowl of kibbles. Sure enough, when he came across the piece with the pill, he'd swallow the meat and spit out the pill.

Not to be outwitted, I bought liverwurst. Pete loved it and would gulp down an entire spoonful without chewing it. Once I found the right vehicle, it was smooth sailing. Unfortunately, it didn't do much for the allergies.

To this day, I wonder how or why Pete ended up with diabetes. He had been a healthy boy, then his pancreas suddenly stopped producing insulin. Did he eat something poisonous when he foraged in the woods at dad's house? Did one of his vaccines cause an autoimmune reaction. Did his mast cell tumor metastasize? I'll never know. But I learned that it is a huge challenge to provide appropriate care for a sick animal. And it doesn't come cheap.

Rule #8:

Make Appropriate Decisions

Obviously, a wise dog owner will make sure that a particular breed fits his or her lifestyle, home, family, and neighborhood. A large dog needs a lot of space, a sporting dog needs a lot of exercise, and a barker is not conducive to peace in the local community.

For some reason, I have never been too smart about my choices. I tended to choose animals that were cute, rather than the best fit. It's kind of like how I would bet on a horse on the very few occasions I went to the race track. The pretty names usually caught my attention. You know, names like *Dusty Rose, Morning Starlight.* or *Aztec Sunset.* My selections never won.

The first puppy I purchased was a darling little miniature poodle. I didn't know anything about poodles, but they look like a cuddly bundle of fur. I did hear that they don't shed too much, and that sounded like a nice feature. I took a walk through the pet store, and my heart was captured as soon as I saw Heidi. I bought her on the spot, as well as a kennel, bowls, food, leash, treats, and a few toys for good measure.

Heidi was a pretty little thing, but she wasn't very smart. I'd put her on the leash and walk her all around the block. "Pee here," I'd say. Nothing. "How about over here?" Nothing. As soon as I brought her in, she'd promptly pee on the rug.

Same thing with the poops. She'd wake me up to go out at 4 a.m. There I was in my jammies, wondering if any of the neighbors were awake and watching this ridiculous routine. Sure enough, Heidi wouldn't do a thing outside. Only when I brought her back to the house. I wasn't happy.

Heidi was a yapper, and she barked incessantly. I may have been annoyed with Pete's bark, but at least it was manly, and it wasn't constant. Heidi drove me crazy. When I left for school in the morning, I'd put her in the crate. I could hear her yapping as I pulled out of the garage. I'd come home for lunch to let her out, and I could hear her barking and crying as soon as I got to my driveway. Same thing after school.

By the fourth day, I'd had enough. I put an ad in the paper the very next day and found a nice family who wanted her and promised to give her a good home. They got a bargain. Heidi and all her stuff for pennies on the dollar. But it was worth it.

When I was growing up, I didn't pay much attention to our various dogs. It's not like I didn't like them. I did. But I wasn't into the cuddling or romping thing.

Our first dog was a female German Shepherd. We named her Lady. Lady was barely out of puppyhood when we had to give her away. My brothers and the neighbor boy were playing soldiers with Lady, and she was a little too aggressive with one of the boys. Sayonara, Lady.

Our next dog was a beagle named Dusty. Beagles are nice. I don't remember too much about Dusty, except that he was a gentle boy. He was quiet and took things as they came. No one had to walk Dusty. In those days, you just opened the door in the morning, and the dog would return to the side porch when he was ready. Could be all day.

I remember a time when my mother's father was visiting, and they were going to the store. As mom backed the car out of the garage, she stopped. My grandfather asked her if there was a problem.

She said, "Something must be on the driveway." He said, "Must be one of the kids' toys. Gun it." Sadly, it was Dusty. Sayonara, Dusty.

When we moved to England, we got a golden Labrador retriever named Rusty. He was a nice boy, but I don't remember much about him either. He was happiest around children and would cozy up with my brothers and sister on the floor when we were watching TV. My sister always fell asleep on him, while sucking her fingers and rubbing his fur. We couldn't take him back to the states when dad's tour of duty was done, so we found a loving home for him with one of the officers on base. Sayonara, Rusty.

When the family moved to Lebanon, Illinois, we got a male golden cocker spaniel. Dad named him Sir Moses of Lebanon, but we called him Mo. He was AKC registered. A few years later, we got a female golden cocker spaniel in Rome, New York. Since my parents planned to breed the cockers, we looked in the family Bible to find the name of Moses' wife. It's Sephora. The female cocker was named Lady Sephora of Rome. We called her Sephie.

When Dad retired from the Air Force, my parents and the three youngest kids returned to Pennsylvania. They built a nice colonial home on the ten acres of land. It was the perfect place to begin breeding Mo and Sephie.

I was surprised that my mother was totally on board with the idea. She would often tell me what she planned to buy when they sold the puppies. New carpet in the dining room. A new living room set.

I remember when Sephie went into labor. Mom had a large carton set up in the laundry room, and she had fitted it with some fluffy towels. She checked often to make sure that Sephie was OK. I was in the family room when mom called out that the first puppy was coming. As I was walking to the laundry room, I heard mom say, "Bad girl, Sephie. You're a bad girl." The first puppy was black, as were the others of the litter. No new carpet. No new living room set. Apparently, Sephie preferred the mutt down the road instead of Mo. Mom decided that the puppy breeding days were over.

Since Dad's plan was that *we* would breed Pete, I imagined that I would someday get a female springer. After she and Pete mated, I'd have a large carton in my kitchen that I would line with towels, and I'd have cute little springer spaniel puppies to sell. I remember thinking that I, too, could use new carpet and a new living room set.

I asked my vet if he knew any owners of female springer spaniels. I figured Pete might need some practice with the girls, so I could rent him out as a stud. The vet didn't know of any. I checked the paper and looked at the notices on the bulletin board in the post office. None. In fact, I realized, there didn't seem to be any springers in the area. No wonder Pete's groomer didn't know how to do a springer cut.

In time, I realized that breeding would not be a good decision, though I occasionally toyed with the idea. What would I do with a bunch of puppies when I had to go to school each day? I decided that it might be better to wait until I was retired. I kept Pete intact, just in case.

I asked Pete's first vet why most dog owners neuter their dogs. He told me the advantages and disadvantages, especially for male dogs. He said that neutering often reduces aggression in males, as well as decreasing the urge to hump furniture or people. There's also less marking of territory with pee. Pete had never been aggressive, except the one time that he attacked Goliath in order to protect me. He never humped unless he was playing with Goliath. And he never marked in the house, though he was pretty adept at it along the fence line in the yard.

I take that back. Pete once marked after Harvey marked in our basement. I made a big to-do about it and told Harvey he had to go home. Pete never did it again in the house. I decided that Pete didn't need neutering.

Once Pete developed diabetes, though, I figured that there would be no puppy breeding. No new carpet, no new living room set. It wouldn't be ethical to sell puppies if the sire had a genetic disposition to diabetes.

By then, however, Pete was mature. I thought he'd really miss his privates. I'm not a guy, but the thought of castration made me cringe. My niece would say, "Snip, snip!" I'd say, "No way. Pete wouldn't like that." After all, Pete liked licking "down there." I stuck to my guns. No neutering.

Once we sold my dad's home with the ten acres, Pete no longer had a place to run. I took him to the local doggie park. The sign said that dogs must be neutered, but I figured no one would notice Pete's equipment, despite being pretty obvious. I ignored the sign and we went in anyway.

It was a large park, totally fenced, with lots of trees and benches. Bags were provided for waste, and you could let your dog off the leash. Pete sniffed the other dogs, while the owners stood around talking. Pete marked every tree. And then he found a friend. A male friend. A large dog like Goliath.

Pete began humping his new friend in earnest. The owner said, "Your dog's not neutered?

You're not supposed to come here with an intact dog." He wasn't mean about it, he was just saying.

Pete was panting. The other dog seemed to like Pete's attention. The owner threw some water on the dogs. My horny dog was totally engaged, though not quite in the right location. We got them apart and I left with Pete. My tail between my legs. We didn't go to the park any more.

I had always thought my decisions were appropriate, but they were unfounded. In other words, a decision is a conclusion or resolution after thinking about different possibilities. I made my decisions without considering the ramifications. They were probably gut reactions, rather than thoughtful choices. In some cases, I made my determinations based on what I *felt* would be suitable. Sometimes the resolutions weren't so simple.

When he was 9 years old, Pete developed a perianal adenoma, a benign tumor, on his privates. His vet explained to me that the tumor grows with testosterone and it can become malignant. She said she could remove the tumor and neuter him at the same time. And she strongly recommended it.

It was such a big decision. I had been adamant that Pete would remain intact. But now it became a health issue. I didn't know what to do. The tumor was growing, and Pete would often lick it or ask for powder.

It was time. "Snip, snip."

I didn't know that Pete would return from the doggie hospital with a large plastic cape around his neck. It got caught on every piece of furniture in the house, and Pete could no longer reach to drink from the toilet. He was miserable. I had to hold a bowl for him to eat and another for him to drink. I knew that the horrible monstrosity was to protect his incision from licking, but there had to be a better way.

I went to the pet store and found an inflatable tube that could be used instead of the plastic cape. It was not cheap, but it seemed more humane. I know. A fool and his money soon part.

After the surgery, I was surprised to see that Pete had a large empty sack hanging between his legs. The vet explained that it would shrink over time. I was happy for Pete that he still had some vestige of his maleness. I had thought the vet would cut off everything.

Pete seemed happy with the results. In fact, my fear that he would miss his privates after all those years was unfounded. He was quite content as a eunuch. The only difference I noticed was that he peed like a girl doggie. No big deal.

Rule #9:

Determine Your Priorities

I suppose, in some way, that I was looking for companionship when I got Pete. I could probably say the same about Heidi, but she wasn't a good fit. As for Jack, I was trying to do my civic duty. That didn't work at all.

I wanted a pet to fill the void and be good company. I'm allergic to cats, so a kitty wouldn't work. I'm probably allergic to dogs, too. If I didn't wash my hands after petting Pete, my eyes would tear up terribly. But cat dander has me sneezing unmercifully. So, getting a dog for company was paramount. I didn't care what kind of dog.

Another priority was for me to get exercise. Getting a dog would get me off the couch and help me get fit. I pictured myself meeting new people on my walks. Finding pleasant camaraderie in my new locale. This went along with the companionship concept, as well. I could kill two birds with one stone. Figuratively.

I forgot that walking the dog meant that you had to do it in the rain, snow, and on a bitterly cold day. I pictured a dog that would walk nicely by my side, not pull me down the road. My idea of walking the dog did not include falling on the ice and breaking a leg. That didn't happen, but I was worried it would. I did meet my neighbors, but some didn't seem to like animals.

On one of our walks, shortly after getting Pete, I was chatting with a new neighbor. Pete didn't want to stand around. He wanted to explore. I gave him plenty of leash, so he didn't have to stand still. After a while, I noticed that there was no longer any pull. No tugs of impatience. I looked around and there was no Pete. Mr. Smarty Pants had chewed through my nice, new leash. I found Pete down the hill at the river's edge. You can't fix retractable leashes that have been chewed through. It went into the trash with the travel crate.

Besides the priorities of companionship and exercise, I also didn't want a dirty house. Quite honestly, I didn't think of that—except in terms of not letting any animal on the furniture. And you know how *that* went.

We had dogs when I was a child and we didn't have a dirty house. Now that I'm older and wiser, I know that's because my mother was an impeccable house cleaner. She even washed windows and wiped out the oven. Things I rarely do. To this day, I blame her for false advertising. She made owning a family dog look easy. I know better now. If a clean house is a big priority, think twice before adopting a pet. A manicured home is not going to happen.

I didn't want a show dog. I wanted a house pet. Show dogs have all sorts of training. I know that I didn't train Pete to be the perfect dog, but I did try. One Christmas, my sister gave me an entire season of *The Dog Whisperer* on DVD's. I watched every single episode and tested each of the lessons on Pete.

I learned that the trick for teaching a dog not to get on the furniture is to maintain a role as alpha figure. You don't just tell your animal to get down; you make him submissive. Not through cruelty or anger, of course. It just happens in the animal kingdom when who's the boss has been determined.

I remembered how Pete reacted to Kayla, when she didn't want him to come near her. Yes, she growled, but there was some kind of silent doggie talk that went on in the scenario. Pete would get down on his belly with his nose to the ground, totally submissive.

I tried that trick with Pete, so he wouldn't get up on the bed. The owner (me) had to get out of bed and point to the floor. "Down." Having the dog sit isn't good enough. That's not doggie submissive. Say it again. "Down." This behavior continues until the dog is lying submissive on the floor. "Stay." The owner (me) gets back in bed. Doggie stays on the floor. If the dog tries to get back on the bed, or should I say *when* the dog returns to the bed, the owner (me) must do it again.

It clearly didn't work with Pete, mostly because I ran out of patience. It was easier for me to invest in a body pillow to keep Pete on his side of the bed. Besides, I didn't want a show dog.

One of the neighbors I met on our walks had a Bichon. Cutest little thing. I only knew that my neighbor had a dog because the lady invited me over to her house. Her doggie was not allowed outside. Never. She was trained to use a kitty litter box. While that sounded like an attractive arrangement, I felt sorry for the dog. She never saw the light of day.

Another lady in my neighborhood had a collie who never had a hair out of place. The dog, not the lady. Pete liked the dog. It was a male, and he liked Pete. But they were not allowed to play because the owner didn't want him to get dirty.

It's important to determine your priorities. Do you want a show dog or a house pet? Do you want a pristinely clean home or a lived-in abode? Once you make your decision, you'll know your expectations for doggie behavior.

Many people choose to get a dog for protection. That was not one of my priorities, although I ended up with a good watch dog. Visitors didn't know that Pete was a wimp. He could hear someone approaching long before I did and would bark to signal their arrival.

As you know, Pete's bark was annoying to me, but I now recognize that it was a good thing. I could sleep in peace with my window open, even though my bedroom is on the ground floor. I could have extra light in the living room by keeping my front door open, using just the storm door to keep out the bugs, because Pete always told me if we had a visitor. Of course, sometimes he was alerting me to animals like squirrels and birds on the patio, but that was OK.

Planned or not, I recognized that having a watchdog was a good thing. It became particularly apparent when Pete was in the doggie hospital. I opened my bedroom window and got into bed. As I was turning out the light, I had second thoughts. What if I didn't hear if someone was outside my window while I was sleeping? I got up and closed the window, locking it for good measure. I locked my storm door, too. Better to be safe than sorry. A watchdog isn't a bad idea. If it's a priority, choose the right breed. Or hope you get as lucky as I did.

Another priority may be a dog's bloodline. Do you want a mutt, or do you want a purebred? It didn't really matter to me, though I always thought a purebred was better. I mean it's important if a dog is AKC registered, right?

I once bragged that Pete had papers and cost only $100. My friend laughed hysterically. "What's so funny?" I asked.

"You may have paid $100 now, but wait until later," he said. "Vet bills, food, medicine, grooming, new furniture, carpet cleaning..." he rambled on.

I now know what he meant. Maintaining a dog is really expensive. I had no idea. Add on Pete's insulin at almost $150 a vial, which lasted only 30 days, and you get my point. Because of in-breeding, purebreds often have more serious health issues, my vet told me. Diabetes can be one of these. Unless you plan to breed or show, bloodline probably isn't a major priority.

Do you travel frequently? Are you often away from home? These questions might help you decide if you want a dog or a more independent pet that doesn't need as much socialization. These weren't priorities I considered when I got Pete. I liked to travel but didn't do it that frequently. And I worked, but I was usually home by 5 p.m., if not sooner. So, no big deal. Besides, I figured, there are kennels if you want to go away.

Pete was always waiting at the door when I returned from school. I noticed that he was particularly clingy and wouldn't leave my side from the moment I got home. I had previously enjoyed going out in the evenings, but Pete would give me the saddest stare as if to say, "Are you kidding me? You're going to leave me again?" I decided it wasn't fair to him that he'd be alone day and night. Instead, we made the evenings his play time.

I had an opportunity to go to a conference in Hawaii, a state I'd never seen. I wrestled with the idea of boarding Pete at a kennel. I knew Pete would be miserable because he'd have to stay in a cage, something he dreaded. My fault. I was ready to decline, but a friend offered to stay at my house, so I could go. It was an amazing experience. When I returned, Pete dashed around the house literally jumping for joy. I was smothered in doggie kisses. He must have thought I had abandoned him and he wasn't about to let that happen again.

It was my priority to have a contented dog. Springers have some unique ways of showing their delight. Pete often had me laughing out loud with his antics. The happy dance was one of them. He'd hop up and down on all four legs, shaking his head to some rhythm he felt. Pete would do his happy dance if he found a special feather in the yard or if I gave him an exceptionally large bone. He'd toss his prize into the air over and over, until he'd finally lie across it, keeping it in stealth mode.

Ownership was clearly established for things other than bones or feathers. I began to notice when Pete was playing outside with his friends that he'd pee on anything he considered his booty. It struck my funny bone every time. Other animals obeyed Pete's claim to proprietorship, but people were not as impressed. For example, when my nephews were playing with Pete's frisbee in the yard, Pete lifted his leg and covered his toy with a stream of urine. The kids screamed in disgust, "Ewww!" And they never touched Pete's frisbee again.

I came to understand that contentment was also demonstrated by the "springer sprawl."

Usually this meant that Pete would lie on his back with his legs and arms wide open, sound asleep. Sometimes snoring. Typically taking up most of the sofa, ¾ of the bed, or an entire upholstered chair. All body parts had to be displayed for the world to see. It was actually very sweet to observe such an open display of total comfort, especially since I've learned that it's typical springer behavior.

Now that Pete has gone to doggie heaven, I'm able to travel and go out in the evenings. Strangely, they're no longer of interest to me. Perhaps Pete and I settled into that routine together. Maybe Pete became my excuse to stay home. Regardless, it was my priority to have a happy, sociable, and well-behaved dog. Whatever I did to achieve my goal, it worked. For both of us.

Rule #10:

Be Consistent

We all like some semblance of consistency in our lives, and our pets are no different. Having a schedule for feeding routines, pit stops, and sleep times gives your dog a sense of security. Of course, our lives can be busy or frenetic, and there are occasions when we don't know if we're coming or going. However, if we make a commitment to owning a dog, we need to be aware of our responsibilities.

A springer spaniel is a high energy dog, especially in its younger years. Obviously, I didn't know that before I got Pete. In my mind, a springer was in the class of a beagle or cocker spaniel, like Dusty or Mo and Sephie. They were quiet dogs who liked to cozy up with us kids on the living room carpet. Even the springer in Dad's picture was snoozing at the old man's feet. Pete preferred a house full of people over just him and me. I know because he told me so.

Intuitively, I knew that Pete needed regular feeding times. I'd always fed him a scoop of dry kibbles in the morning before I left for school. He'd eat a little of it but saved most for when I came home. Pete would get an extra scoop of dry kibbles at supper time, and I always mixed in some leftover meat. He was usually ravenous, as he got good exercise playing with Damien or Goliath, and he'd gobble down his entire bowl of food. In the evening, Pete would get a special treat like a rawhide bone that he could spend time chewing on.

Pete and I kept to that routine, until dad had a stroke and Pete got diabetes. Despite trying to keep some kind of stability as I helped care for dad, I found it easier to buy hot dogs and frozen chicken nuggets that could be zapped in the microwave. Bad choice for Pete and for me. I bought those little packets of moist dog food and Pete wolfed them down along with the fast food. Little did I know that everything he was eating was loaded with high fructose corn syrup. He loved it, and I thought he was getting the nutrients he needed.

Once Pete's diabetes and ulcer were detected, the vet put him on the special diet and recommended no more rawhide bones. I found a brand of treats that had no sugar and would give him those as a reward for letting me inject his insulin. Since the insulin made Pete hungry all the time, he begged constantly. Not a good routine.

To counteract Pete's voracious appetite, I found a high protein, high nutrient chicken and rice kibbles mixture that had no sugar, and I added baked skinless chicken at breakfast and supper. I only included steamed rice if Pete seemed to have an upset stomach. We tried a can of diabetic dog food suggested by the vet, but Pete refused to eat it. Other varieties of canned dog food and kibbles seemed to trigger vomiting or diarrhea, even though he liked them. Finding the right balance wasn't easy.

I was lucky that Pete wasn't in a hurry to go out early in the morning. Occasionally, if his blood sugar was high, Pete would wake me up in the middle of the night to tell me he had to pee. Otherwise, he preferred to sleep in, sprawled across the bed like he hadn't a care in the world.

My friend's dog, on the other hand, always got her up in the wee hours of the morning. She'd let him out, fix his breakfast, and crawl back to bed for 2 more hours of sleep. Not Pete, thank goodness.

He was quite content to watch me sleep, then wait for me to get dressed. I'd like to think that I trained him that way.

Poops were another story. Unless you teach your dog to use the litter box as my neighbor did, reliability with #2 can be a challenge. When Pete was a puppy and we took those walks to the river many times a day, I would always plan for Pete to have a pit stop in my own yard first. You already know how that went.

Pete wanted only to see his friends and had no interest in bodily functions. Except to pee on every bush along the way. Invariably, he would do his business when we got to Ross's yard. No problem. With three dogs of his own, the backyard was a minefield. Literally. But he had nice fertile soil and the grass was luxuriant.

Of course, Pete's regularity only lasted until the new people forbade the dogs to be loose. Then I had to find a conducive spot for Pete. My specifications for where to go were not the same as his. I thought our yard would be perfect. Pete didn't seem to agree.

A new house was being built across the street and the owners wanted some fertilizer for landscaping their lawn. They suggested that I encourage Pete do his business there, reminding me that dogs don't like to go in their own territory.

That did the trick. Instead of wandering in circles trying to find the perfect spot, we'd just cross the street and Bingo. Fast and easy, and I didn't have to pick it up. That worked well until the first owners decided they didn't want the house.

They sold the place to a young couple who must not have been pet lovers. I came home from school one day to find them using a snow shovel to throw all of Pete's poops into my front yard. I don't know if all springers pass big plops like Pete, but they were quite distinctive. I tried to explain that we were invited to use their yard. They were not nice about it.

I now had a serious consistency dilemma. Pete wouldn't use our yard, and he wasn't allowed across the street or down by the river. I began to walk him to a large field behind the mean people's house, making sure to carry a pooper scooper and bag in clear sight.

Unfortunately, Pete didn't find it to be an appropriate location. He would walk around in circles on the leash, with me following after him, then decide there was a better place. Around and around we went.

"How about here?" I'd say. "Do some poops!" I'd remind him. Once he had his smell in the area, everything came out fine. Until the guy who owned the land came by on his tractor to mow the grass. He told us to get out of his field and not come back. It didn't matter that I carried the evidence of Pete's business in the bag.

It was clearly time to fence my yard and get a doggie door. Do you know how much it costs to have fencing, gates, and doggie doors installed? Regardless, it was the best investment I could have made. I no longer needed to find a suitable location or walk in circles until Pete found his spot. He was on his own and all I had to do was pick up all the poops on trash day. It made life so much easier.

I wish I could say that once we achieved stability with doggie hygiene, we were able to maintain it. Unfortunately, that was not the case. During dad's illness, Pete and I were nomads, travelling back and forth that 3-hour drive to share in the care-giving. After dad's death, I put my home on the market and lived at dad's house until I could find my own place. Pete roamed the ten acres and could do his business in the woods. He loved it.

I eventually found the perfect place for me, but Pete only had a small fenced patio. It wasn't ideal, but it included some bushes and perennials around the perimeter, and that was a perfect spot for Pete to pee. There were also lots of trees and green space surrounding my unit, and I was able to rig up a rope, so he could go there to poop. Of course, I made sure that all of the neighbors saw me with the pooper scooper and bag.

So, here's the message. When you get a dog, any breed, plan ahead for how you'll handle day to day tasks in a consistent manner. Recognize that a springer spaniel has specific needs that include proper nutrients, lots of exercise, and appropriate personal hygiene. Involve your dog in activities that stimulate healthy behavior.

A few years ago, someone asked if I had a pet. When I replied that I had a springer spaniel, she gasped. She told me that her sister had owned a springer who was completely destructive. The dog ate the furniture, chewed the rug, pulled off moldings along the walls. I don't believe that's typical springer behavior. Pete had never done any of those things. The worst thing Pete ever did was scratch my door frame that first night when I brought him to my home and wouldn't let him into my bedroom.

Maybe I've been lucky, or maybe I intuitively knew that Pete needed the stimulation of being involved. I'd often say to him, "Can you help me take the trash to the garage?" or "Do you want to help me feed the birds?" Pete could be sound asleep on the sofa, but when he heard the word "help," he jumped up to assist me. If I'd spill some water, I'd say, "Get me the towel." He'd go right to the oven door and bring me the dishcloth. Of course, he'd tease me with it until he got a treat. That's how I trained him.

Consistency is also relevant to maintaining discipline. Once you determine what is acceptable behavior in your dog, don't change the rules. In my case, I hadn't planned to permit Pete on furniture or the bed. As you know, Pete had a different view. But I found that I liked him to rest his head on my lap when I watched TV. Though he was never allowed under the covers in the bed, it was nice getting into a bed already warmed with his radiant body heat. Changing the routine on my mood or whims would have made Pete nervous, maybe even neurotic.

Based on the experience I had when the dog warden stood with my front door open, Pete was told to only use the doggy door when he wanted to go out. If we were in the fenced yard, and I went out the gate, he was to stay. If he was helping me bring in the groceries with the garage door open, he was to follow me into the house. I'm not sure how Pete learned that rule so quickly, but he was respectful of it. I'd like to think that it was because of my training, but it may have been because of a situation we had when he was still young.

One evening, late fall, I was making supper in the kitchen. Pete was snoozing in the living room, or so I thought. At one point, I went into the garage to put garbage in the bin, then returned to continue my task. Later, I turned on the TV and noticed that Pete wasn't in his usual spot on the sofa. I checked the bedroom and bathroom. No Pete. Thinking he might have gone out to the yard, I stood on the darkened deck and called his name. No Pete. My neighbors returned from an outing, their car lights shining in my yard. No Pete. They joined me in the search and I began to panic as all three of us were calling him. Finally, we heard a distant yelp from inside the garage. Pete must have followed me when I put out the garbage. He saturated me with wet kisses when I rescued him. Maybe it taught him a lesson. Except for using the doggie door, Pete never went outside without me again.

Pete was never permitted to take food from the kitchen counter. When he was large enough, he could reach his front paws up and check out the lay of the land, so to speak. I'd say, "Don't even think about it," and he'd get down. Pete tried it one time when my sister was visiting, and she smacked his nose. That seemed to do the trick. Until one day when I zapped chicken nuggets in the microwave. I had added a few extra on the plate as I knew he'd be begging for some. They were too hot, so I left them to cool on the counter. Pete followed me to the bedroom where I was folding clothes. When I finished, I said, "Let's go get our nuggets." The plate was empty! Still on the counter, exactly where I had left it, not a morsel was left. Somehow Pete had snuck away and ate every one of them. But he knew what he had done was wrong. He held his head in shame, his tail wagging profusely. At least Pete said he was sorry.

I don't know how I knew that consistency was so important when raising a puppy. Perhaps because it was a method I used in the classroom to minimize disruptive behavior. Maybe it's just the way my parents raised me. I knew my boundaries and I knew the consequences of not following rules. Regardless, it works for people and for doggies. Maintaining a stable environment is an important principle to follow.

Rule #11:
Know Your Limitations

Raising a springer spaniel is an enormous commitment of time and resources. Based on my experience, a springer would make an excellent family dog. Pete was very sociable and liked having people around. He adored the attention and the belly rubs that visitors provided. In fact, he never hesitated to cozy up with guests and stretch out on his back to afford easy access.

Springers do seem to get attached to people, particularly one who is the main caregiver. Pete followed me around constantly. When I'd do the laundry, he was at my side. If I went to the bedroom for something, he followed me. If he heard the crinkling of a cheese wrapper, he was at my feet.

Time had no boundaries when living with Pete. Now that Pete's no longer with me, I'm amazed at the amount of time that revolved around him. If Pete wanted to go out at dad's house or our new home, I had to go with him. He made sure I was there, never letting me out of his sight. When Pete would let me know there had been a recent squirrel or bird on the tree, I'd have to give the appropriate response. Such was the case wherever we lived. He'd always check to make sure that I was on the deck or porch or patio. I'm not sure if that's true for all springers, but I know that Pete was very attached to me. He was also a wimp.

As a puppy, before we had a fenced yard, I'd walk endlessly with Pete to and from the river while he played with his friends. Once we had the yard and Goliath would visit, it was important for me to be there as well. I'd try to use that time for chores or gardening, or talking with neighbors over the fence, but it was time-consuming. And when Pete had no yard, I'd drive him to the dog park or a grassy field, so he had a place to frolic. I don't regret one moment because, in the long run, I benefited as much as Pete did. But, if your time is limited, do yourself a favor. Don't invest in a dog, regardless of the breed, that will end up alone in an empty house or cage. Dogs need companionship, socialization, and opportunity to run. Find yourself a pet that is more independent.

I learned how expensive it is to own a dog. When Pete was a puppy, I'd buy him a toy whenever I went shopping. He'd play with it the first day, then it would lay unattended to litter the living room carpet. Eventually, I got a large container to store his toys. When I got home from school, I'd make a great fuss of removing the lid to bring out a toy I thought would be entertaining. I liked the stuffed animals that squeaked. Pete, not so much. He'd sniff at my find, then walk away. It didn't matter if it was a colorful bird or a fluffy squirrel. Pete wasn't fooled. Those weren't real animals and he didn't like them.

I began buying the cheapie rubber toys that squeaked. Pete found them more captivating, but would soon tire of them, too. The toy box was beyond full. I was amazed to find that Pete's biggest interest was bird feathers or discarded cartons, gift bags, and paper towel rolls. He'd shake those things around for hours, and then start to tear them apart. Pete was quite adept at ripping off big pieces and spitting them out. I'd watch him carefully to make sure he didn't swallow any bits, but then I had a mess of torn cardboard to clean up. I realized that I no longer needed to spend money on toys. In fact, I gave most of his playthings away or put them in the yard for his friends. Eventually, they ended up in the trash.

I probably went overboard with trying to stimulate Pete. He didn't need or want all of the things I bought. He was quite content playing with boxes and chasing real squirrels. I cringe at the amount of money I wasted, as well as the cost of the necessities of dog ownership. If you don't have financial stability, it's better to find a less expensive pet. I'm not saying that we need to be wealthy to afford a dog. But we do need to be able to manage our day-to-day expenses.

One of my neighbors was a single mom on disability with a teenage son. She thought that her boy might get over his desire to have a dog if he saw how much work was involved. She asked if her son could take Pete on walks each day to learn that he'd have to be responsible for picking up the poop and properly disposing it. Within a very short time, the teen no longer showed much interest in Pete. Despite his lack of attention to Pete, my neighbor eventually bought a large breed of dog, still a puppy, for her son. That pup had paws the size of my hand, and he was extremely energetic. Pete didn't take to him and would bark whenever he saw him. Not the high pitched, "Let's play," kind of bark. It was a grumpy bark.

My point is that this woman was struggling to make ends meet. That puppy was going to be big, and just feeding him properly would cost a lot of money. The teen soon tired of walking his dog, too, so the puppy was left chained in the yard. My heart broke for him. We're no longer neighbors, but I often wonder how long they were able to keep the dog. Clearly, they didn't consider their limitations.

I didn't give enough reflection to the aging process when I got Pete. I recognized that Pete would be a commitment for a number of years, but I didn't think about the fact that I, too, would be advancing in age. Just after Pete was diagnosed with diabetes and mast cell cancer, I learned that I had breast cancer and melanoma. I faced chemo and radiation treatments. Pete had surgery to remove his tumor. Both of us were healing and comforting each other while we maintained consistency in our daily routine. It wasn't easy.

And I worried. What would happen to Pete if I passed on to the heavenly abode before he did? I literally had to mull about that as I prepared my last will and testament. Would any of my siblings adopt him? Would Pete adjust to different surroundings? Or would he end up figuratively waiting for me at the train station day after day, like the dog in the movie *Hachi*? Age can certainly be a limitation.

Regardless of our challenges, Pete and I both still needed exercise. I no longer had the energy I'd had when Pete was a puppy. I retired from full-time teaching and took a part-time job teaching on-line. It gave me great flexibility, but I sat for hours at the computer grading assignments. Pete would snooze at my feet. Still, we made time in the afternoons for exercise. I preferred to get mine by swimming at the Y. Pete needed to be walked. Quite honestly, he didn't like being on the leash. He's a field dog, for heaven's sake. He liked nothing better than to be free to explore the surroundings, searching for animals. Although he couldn't run free in our new environment, he had the rigged-up rope on our patio fence. It was a limitation, but it worked.

There's a huge overgrown copse of bushes just beyond the patio gate that is a haven for small critters. I've seen bunnies, squirrels, birds, and groundhogs scurrying in and out of the thicket. Pete knew they were there, and that's the first place he wanted to explore when we'd go out. I put him on the rope and watched him peer into the bushes. The rope was long enough for him to explore the perimeter, but he couldn't get too far in. I figured the animals were safe until one day I noticed that Pete seemed to be playing with something. Pete was doing the happy dance he'd do whenever he found an interesting bird feather.

I went to investigate and discovered that Pete had caught a groundhog. He looked up at me with a big smile and a proud look on his face. I didn't share his enthusiasm. Instead, I grunted my disdain. "Oh, yuck, Pete. What did you do?" The groundhog looked dead, but there were no visible signs of trauma. I got the shovel from the garage, bagged the deceased animal, and put him in the dumpster. Pete was very upset. Strangely, the groundhog was soft. *Rigor mortis* hadn't set in. I thought that was strange.

A friend explained that groundhogs play dead if they're caught. Uh oh. The poor critter met an early demise—on my account, not Pete's. Anyway, Pete was not happy with me at all. He stomped into the house and hid in his cave behind the recliner. And I felt sad about the animal I had apparently smothered in the trash bag.

Dogs make a great family pet. I hadn't thought about the limitation for Pete that it would just be Pete and me. I'm boring. Well, maybe not from a people perspective, but definitely from a dog's perspective. I have to give myself credit for the time I devoted to making sure that Pete had daily socialization and companionship. I involved him in all of the household activities such as doing the laundry and taking out the trash. But I didn't often play ball or frisbee with him because of his enthusiastic bark. I should have worked on that more when he was a puppy. Nonetheless, Pete would have enjoyed having other people around.

I hadn't thought about the limitations of doggie ownership before getting Pete. But it's an important consideration. We certainly can't plan everything we might encounter in life. Wouldn't that be a drag? Just make sure to choose wisely. Make sure you have the time, resources, and energy to properly care for the breed of dog you select. I lucked out in many respects. Springers are so loyal and smart, Pete was the perfect pet for me. In fact, if—or when—I get another dog, it will be a springer spaniel. I'm sure of it!

Rule #12:

Inevitable Challenges

Pete and I settled into a new stage of reality after his diagnosis of diabetes and my bout with cancer. Both of us adjusted our lifestyle, but neither of us wallowed in pity. Life went on, and it was good.

I noticed Pete slowing down after his neutering. He was quite content to snooze much of the day away, no longer springing from sofa to chair, not interested in finding animals outside. Many days, he'd just sleep at my feet when I worked on the computer or lay his head on my lap if I watched TV.

We took a walk each morning, and a drive many afternoons, stopping to chat with neighbors along the way. Pete was more active in the evenings, I observed, but that had been his pattern as a puppy, so I wasn't concerned.

In 2016, I had spinal surgery, then a knee replacement. My sister convinced me that I should hire a dog-walker. Pete liked his new friend and would lie on the floor by the front door awaiting her arrival each morning. He initially enjoyed exploring paths through the woods or along the creek. As time went on, though, the walks got shorter. Pete would lead her home, adamant that his stroll with her was done.

More puzzling was Pete's behavior through the night. He'd awaken me, nudging my arm while whimpering and panting. I assumed he had to go out, and I'd struggle with my walker to go open the front door for him. Invariably he'd just head over to the sofa, not at all interested in doing his business.

"Why'd you wake me up?" I'd scold, heading back to bed. But as soon as I'd fall asleep, his panting and whimpering began anew.

I called the vet to see if she'd prescribe some sort of sedative for his strange behavior. She insisted that I bring Pete in for a check-up. In two minutes, she had found the cause. Pete was totally blind.

It was amazing to me that Pete showed no sign of his complete blindness. No tripping over furniture, no difficulty finding his spot on the bed or sofa. He even pulled the dog-walker directly to our front door when he tired of his walk.

The vet suggested that Pete's panic through the night was probably due to having his days and nights mixed up. He woke me, she said, because he believed that I shouldn't be sleeping at that time. Perhaps he worried that something was wrong, that I was sick or dying. As usual, Pete was protecting me.

It was important, his vet said, that I set up a well-defined ritual at bedtime. I overemphasized when it was dark and time to close the blinds or turn down the bed. In the morning, I'd announce that the sun was shining, and it was time to get up. Within a week of the new routine, Pete slept through the night.

Once I was able to get around, I no longer needed the services of the dog-walker. Pete and I took his morning walk together, sometimes adding an afternoon stroll. He showed me his favorite spots—the fire hydrant on the corner, the copse of trees up the hill, the path in front of the clubhouse. For the most part, there was no sign of Pete's blindness, though he occasionally tripped up a curb. I became Pete's service person, warning him when he needed to step up or walk around a fallen branch.

Winter set in and we continued our walks unless it was icy. I was grateful that Pete didn't want to stay out very long in the cold. He'd do his business and lead me home. But his digestive problems intensified. And his diabetes was out of control. He vomited often, or had diarrhea, to the point that I no longer knew how much insulin to inject. I was flying by the seat of my pants.

I went back to testing Pete's urine twice a day and adjusted his insulin accordingly. If there was too much glucose, I'd increase his dose. I watched his food intake like a hawk. He began drinking more water and peeing more often. More vomiting. More diarrhea.

By the time March roared in like a lion, Pete had his good days and bad ones. Sometimes he couldn't get up onto the bed, though he learned to maneuver his way by climbing first onto the recliner, then sliding over to the bed. He'd sleep close to me, often resting his head on my arm. I had a horrible feeling that Pete was dying.

I tried to prepare myself, wondering if I'd be able to let Pete go peacefully. I prayed for strength, for wisdom, for courage. Still I told Pete he was doing fine, that he'd get better soon. "Don't worry," I'd say. "You take care of me, and I take care of you."

On March 15, we had a whopper of a snowstorm. It was a winter nor'easter, the kind that drops a couple feet of snow. Pete didn't want to go out, nor did he want to eat. I prepared home-made creamed chicken and rice, thinking it might settle his stomach, and hand-fed him the little bit that he wanted. He slept at my feet all day.

By dusk, Pete told me he needed to go out, but our front door was snowed shut. I opened the garage door and showed him the way. He wandered through the drifts, trying to find a place to poop. I called to him above the howling wind, yet he was totally disoriented. He couldn't hear my voice and his face showed panic. He meandered down the driveway, confused, while I grabbed my boots, all the while yelling "Here, boy. I'm here!"

Suddenly, Pete found his bearings or heard my shouts and returned to the garage. I remember saying, "Whew, that was scary!" He wagged his tail in agreement. After I dried him with the towel, we cuddled on the sofa. He wanted nothing to eat for supper, so I decided to hold off on the insulin.

Two hours later, just as I had opened my on-line class for seminar, Pete dragged himself across the floor and collapsed at my feet. What seemed like a gallon of urine seeped out of him. I ran to get a towel and a test strip, but I couldn't get a decent glucose reading. Pete had passed out, yet he was breathing. I told my class that I thought my dog was dying, struggling to stay focused. It was the longest hour I've ever experienced.

After class, I tried to think through the entire scenario. Pete's confusion, his passing out, his back legs not working were similar to the diabetic crash he'd had several years before. This time was different, though. Because Pete had only eaten the smallest iota of food, I hadn't given him any insulin. Nonetheless, I got out the corn syrup and rubbed it all over Pete's gums and tongue. The inside of his mouth was entirely white. No healthy pink hue.

Pete awoke about 11 p.m. and dragged himself to the front door. I knew we couldn't get it open, trying to explain to Pete that we'd have to go out through the garage. Once again, he passed out, collapsed in another gallon of pee. I began to cry softly, so he wouldn't worry if he heard me. "It's OK, Pete," I said, rubbing his back. "Grandpop's waiting for you in heaven. He'll take care of you."

I sat with Pete at the door for over an hour. He was unconscious but still breathing shallowly. Finally, I turned out the lights and prepared for bed. I was brushing my teeth when Pete appeared. Back legs not working, he had dragged himself from the living room to the bathroom, collapsing at my feet once more. I couldn't lift Pete to the bed, but I checked on him all through the night.

Pete was still breathing in the morning, and his legs were strong enough for him to follow me to the kitchen. I got him some water, but he wanted no food. His gums were still white. He told me he needed to go out, so I opened the garage door. He pooped on the driveway, then sat with a silly grin in the cold snow on the neighbor's sidewalk. I half-carried, half-dragged Pete home, telling him how much I loved him.

It seemed like an eternity before the vet's office opened for the day. She told me to bring Pete in right away. "You want to go to the doctor?" I asked Pete. He wagged his tail in agreement. I retrieved Pete's insulin from the refrigerator. Then he followed me out to the car, doing what he could to help me boost him to the back seat.

When we arrived at the vet's office, one of the staff came out to carry Pete in. There was no fear on Pete's face, just calm relief. A blanket was spread on the floor in the procedure room and Pete was gently placed on it next to me. He wagged his tail when the vet arrived.

She examined Pete while I explained all that had transpired over the last 24 hours. I handed her the vial of insulin, suggesting that maybe it's all he needed to get better. She sadly shook her head, saying that Pete was, in fact, dying. She pointed to his swollen belly and white gums, suggesting that he was bleeding internally. All of his bodily systems had shut down.

In a gentle voice, Pete's vet told me that we could assist his death so that he wouldn't suffer, or I could take him home and wait for the inevitable. It was a choice I had never wanted to make. My mind raced to question how I'd be able to care for Pete. He wouldn't eat; therefore, I wouldn't know how much insulin to administer. We couldn't even get out my front door for him to do his business. And most of all, how would I remove his body when I couldn't lift him?

I chose to help Pete go to heaven. It was a very, very painful decision. The vet administered a sedative, then positioned Pete in the frog-leg way that springers sleep on their bellies. I softly said good-bye, tears falling to my cheeks. Pete closed his eyes, and my best friend was gone.

Bringing Closure

My sister used to say that Pete was spoiled. Heck, everyone said that Pete was spoiled. I disagree. Pete was well aware of his boundaries, and he listened to what I said. Most times. My sister said that Pete was spoiled because I allowed him to beg for food and I gave him too many treats. Well, OK, I agree with that. But, Pete wasn't spoiled. She said that Pete had me wrapped around his little paws. Well, OK, maybe a little. But, Pete wasn't spoiled. My sister said that Pete was spoiled because I allowed him to limit my ability to travel or socialize. Well, it's true that I didn't go out in the evening and preferred not to board Pete at a kennel, but that didn't make him spoiled.

I had a similar discussion with a friend who has always had pets. She often reminded me that Pete was an animal, not a person. I asked Pete if he thought he was "a people." He wagged his tail vehemently. Therein lies the answer. Pete was a "people-doggie." And whether he was spoiled or not, he was a good boy. I'm sure of it, because I trained him that way.

Pete and I were together for a long time. We had been through some rough spells and had to adjust to big changes in our lives. Through it all, I managed to stay sane, and Pete had been my staunchest supporter.

Looking back, would I do things differently? Most certainly. I would research dog breeds to see which was the most compatible with my personality and lifestyle. I would stick with a training regimen to assure that appropriate doggie behaviors were strictly reinforced. I would make sure that my dog conformed to my expectations, not the other way around.

Still, I lucked out. Springer spaniels have unique traits that are quite adorable. Pete was smart. Very smart. Maybe too smart for his own britches. I liked that about him. I liked that he understood what I'd say. I liked that he answered my questions with a wag of his tail. I even liked that

I had to spell words when I spoke with my friends, so he wouldn't know what I was talking about.

Pete was protective of me. I felt safe when he was around. I used to worry that he was a little too attached to me, that he'd languish if I were the first to go. But he was definitely loyal. It's comforting to know that I was loved wholeheartedly and without reservation, despite my foibles.

Pete was adaptable. He managed to adjust to three different environments, and numerous new scenarios. Through the years, he said good-bye to some very close friends, as have I, and he welcomed new acquaintances with gusto. Pete showed me that it's not *where* you live that's important. It's imperative, however, that you open your heart and your home to others.

Pete was resilient. My poor mutt let me stick a needle in his backside twice a day to give him insulin. And I wasn't that good at it, as I learned when his urine showed extremely high sugar and he went blind. Pete endured hospitalization when I didn't realize that he was deathly ill. He put up with castration at a late age because I was too convinced that he might want to make puppies.

Pete was sensitive. He knew when I was sad and when I needed cuddling. He watched me cry at my father's deathbed and comforted me when I learned that I had cancer. Pete showed me that it's

OK to express my feelings. And that things will eventually get better.

I often told Pete that he was a lucky dog. He'd wag his tail to tell me that he knew it. But, quite honestly, I was the lucky one. I had a doggie who taught me more than I could ever imagine.

Dad was right when he told me, "You should get him." And he really did pick the best of the litter. May you be as fortunate as I was.

R.I.P., Sir Peter of Archbald
3.16.17

If you enjoyed reading Pete's story, please consider posting a review on Amazon and/or Goodreads.

Pictures of Pete are available on my website at https://kathleen-mckee.com/pete/

Made in the USA
Middletown, DE
28 October 2020